Learn Today Achieve Tomorrow

School Journal

School Journal

This journal belongs to:

_____

SCHOOL CHECKLIST

A Week Before

- ☐ Practice sleeping and waking routines
- ☐ Purchase school supplies

The Night Before

- ☐ Prepare school clothes
- ☐ Pack your bag, lunch, and snacks
- ☐ Set the alarm clock
- ☐ Go to bed early

First Day of School

- ☐ Have fun!
- ☐ Learn and make new friends

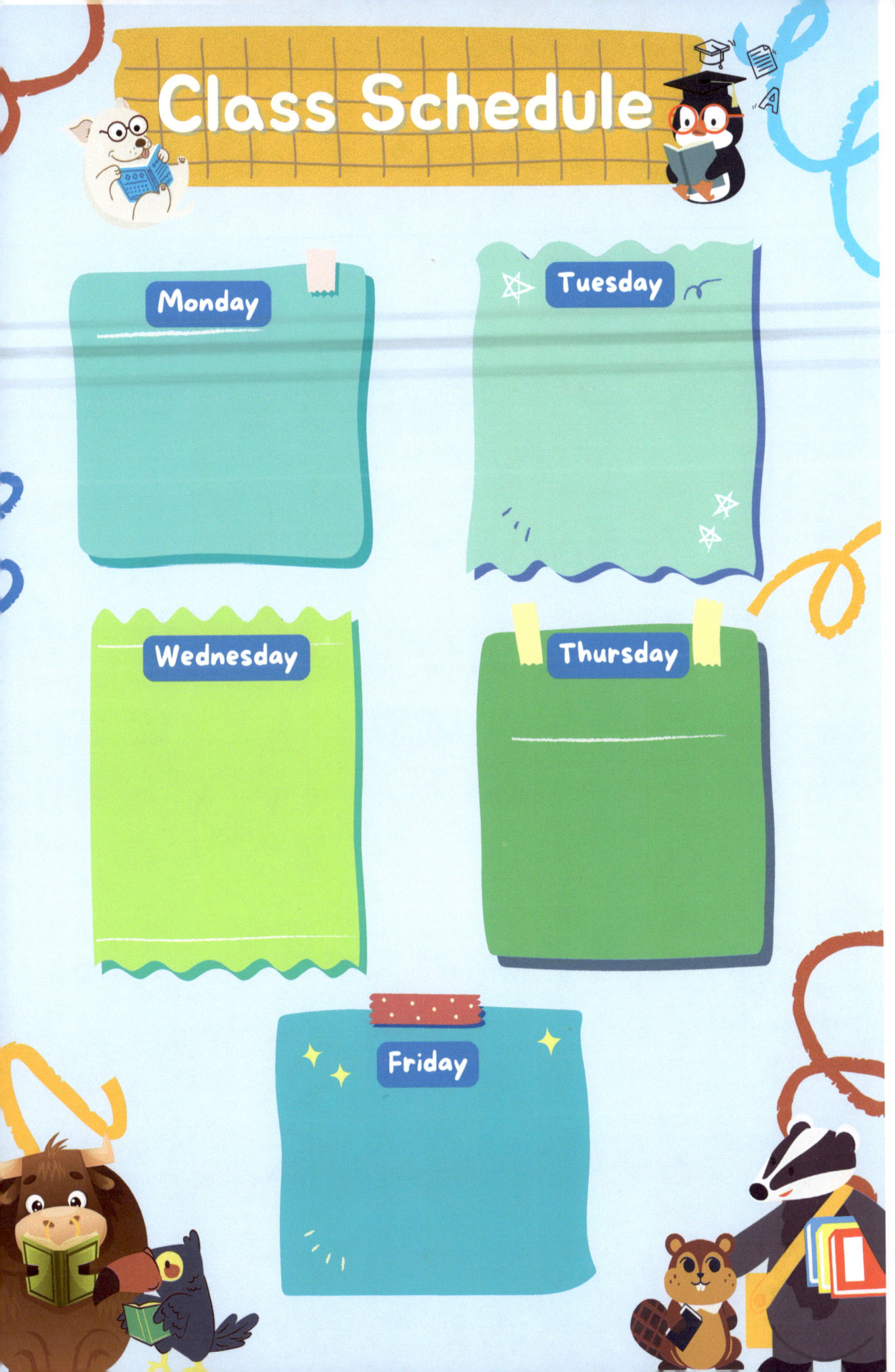

Study Plan

Monday

Tuesday

Wednesday

Thursday

Friday

Weekends

Notes

Study TIPS

- 💡 Get quality sleep
- 💡 Try a new study environment
- 💡 Eliminate distractions
- 💡 Listen to calming music
- 💡 Snack on healthy food
- 💡 Try color-coded notes
- 💡 Exercise before studying
- 💡 Create flash cards from lessons
- 💡 Review your notes frequently
- 💡 Take practice tests

MONTHLY PLANNER

MONTH _____   **YEAR** _____

SUN	MON	TUE	WED	THU	FRI	SAT

TO-DO LIST

-
-
-
-

MONTHLY GOALS

- ☐
- ☐
- ☐
- ☐

WEEKLY PLANNER

WEEK _____ **MONTH** _____

SUNDAY	
MONDAY	
TUESDAY	
WEDNESDAY	
THURSDAY	
FRIDAY	
SATURDAY	

TO DO LIST

-
-
-
-
-
-
-
-
-
-
-
-

TASK PLANNER

S M T W T F S
○ ○ ○ ○ ○ ○ ○

DATE:

TASKS

- ------------------------
- ------------------------
- ------------------------
- ------------------------
- ------------------------
- ------------------------
- ------------------------
- ------------------------
- ------------------------
- ------------------------

PRIORITIES

NOTES

DAILY DIARY

DATE:

S M T W T F S
○ ○ ○ ○ ○ ○ ○

Today's Meals

What did you learn today?

Water intake

What are you grateful for today?

How do you feel today?

Why do you feel this way?

Rate your day!

TASK PLANNER

S M T W T F S
◯ ◯ ◯ ◯ ◯ ◯ ◯

DATE :

TASKS

- _____
- _____
- _____
- _____
- _____
- _____
- _____
- _____
- _____
- _____

PRIORITIES

NOTES

DAILY DIARY

DATE :

S M T W T F S
○ ○ ○ ○ ○ ○ ○

Today's Meals

What did you learn today?

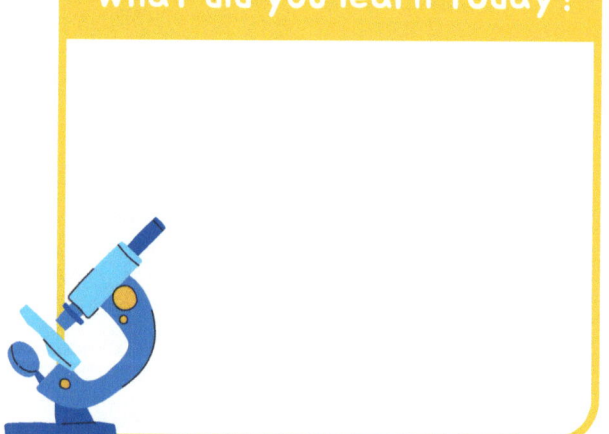

Water intake

What are you grateful for today?

How do you feel today?

Why do you feel this way?

Rate your day!

TASK PLANNER

S M T W T F S
○ ○ ○ ○ ○ ○ ○

DATE:

TASKS

- _____
- _____
- _____
- _____
- _____
- _____
- _____
- _____
- _____
- _____

PRIORITIES

NOTES

DAILY DIARY

DATE:

S M T W T F S
○ ○ ○ ○ ○ ○ ○

Today's Meals

What did you learn today?

Water intake

What are you grateful for today?

How do you feel today?

Why do you feel this way?

Rate your day!

TASK PLANNER

S M T W T F S
○ ○ ○ ○ ○ ○ ○

DATE:

TASKS

PRIORITIES

NOTES

DAILY DIARY

DATE:

S M T W T F S
◯ ◯ ◯ ◯ ◯ ◯ ◯

Today's Meals

What did you learn today?

Water intake

What are you grateful for today?

How do you feel today?

Why do you feel this way?

Rate your day!

TASK PLANNER

S M T W T F S
○ ○ ○ ○ ○ ○ ○

DATE:

TASKS

- ----------------
- ----------------
- ----------------
- ----------------
- ----------------
- ----------------
- ----------------
- ----------------
- ----------------
- ----------------

PRIORITIES

NOTES

DAILY DIARY

DATE: _____

S M T W T F S
○ ○ ○ ○ ○ ○ ○

What did you learn today?

Today's Meals

Water intake

What are you grateful for today?

How do you feel today?

Why do you feel this way?

Rate your day!

TASK PLANNER

S M T W T F S
◯ ◯ ◯ ◯ ◯ ◯ ◯

DATE :

TASKS

- _____
- _____
- _____
- _____
- _____
- _____
- _____
- _____
- _____
- _____

PRIORITIES

NOTES

DAILY DIARY

DATE: _____

S M T W T F S
○ ○ ○ ○ ○ ○ ○

Today's Meals

- ----------
- ----------
- ----------
- ----------

What did you learn today?

Water intake

What are you grateful for today?

How do you feel today?

Why do you feel this way?

Rate your day!

TASK PLANNER

S M T W T F S
○ ○ ○ ○ ○ ○ ○

DATE:

TASKS

- _____
- _____
- _____
- _____
- _____
- _____
- _____
- _____
- _____
- _____
- _____
- _____

PRIORITIES

NOTES

DAILY DIARY

DATE :

S M T W T F S
○ ○ ○ ○ ○ ○ ○

Today's Meals

What did you learn today?

Water intake

What are you grateful for today?

How do you feel today?

Why do you feel this way?

Rate your day!

MONTHLY PLANNER

MONTH _____ **YEAR** _____

SUN	MON	TUE	WED	THU	FRI	SAT

TO-DO LIST

- _____
- _____
- _____
- _____

MONTHLY GOALS

☐ _____
☐ _____
☐ _____
☐ _____

WEEKLY PLANNER

WEEK _____ **MONTH** _____

SUNDAY	
MONDAY	
TUESDAY	
WEDNESDAY	
THURSDAY	
FRIDAY	
SATURDAY	

TO DO LIST
-
-
-
-
-
-
-
-
-
-
-

TASK PLANNER

S M T W T F S
○ ○ ○ ○ ○ ○ ○

DATE:

TASKS

- _____
- _____
- _____
- _____
- _____
- _____
- _____
- _____
- _____
- _____

PRIORITIES

NOTES

DAILY DIARY

DATE: _____

S M T W T F S
○ ○ ○ ○ ○ ○ ○

Today's Meals

What did you learn today?

Water intake

What are you grateful for today?

How do you feel today?
😊 ☹️ 😫 😯 😭 😠

Why do you feel this way?

Rate your day!
☆ ☆ ☆ ☆ ☆

TASK PLANNER

S M T W T F S
○ ○ ○ ○ ○ ○ ○

DATE :

TASKS

PRIORITIES

NOTES

DAILY DIARY

DATE:

S M T W T F S
○ ○ ○ ○ ○ ○ ○

Today's Meals

What did you learn today?

Water intake

What are you grateful for today?

How do you feel today?

🙂 🙁 😫 😯 😭 😠

Why do you feel this way?

Rate your day!

⭐ ⭐ ⭐ ⭐ ⭐

TASK PLANNER

S M T W T F S
○ ○ ○ ○ ○ ○ ○

DATE:

TASKS

- _____
- _____
- _____
- _____
- _____
- _____
- _____
- _____
- _____
- _____

PRIORITIES

NOTES

DAILY DIARY

DATE : _____

S M T W T F S
○ ○ ○ ○ ○ ○ ○

Today's Meals

What did you learn today?

Water intake

What are you grateful for today?

How do you feel today?

😊 🙁 😖 😯 😭 😠

Why do you feel this way?

Rate your day!

☆ ☆ ☆ ☆ ☆

TASK PLANNER

S M T W T F S
○ ○ ○ ○ ○ ○ ○

DATE:

TASKS

PRIORITIES

NOTES

DAILY DIARY

DATE:

S M T W T F S
○ ○ ○ ○ ○ ○ ○

What did you learn today?

Today's Meals

Water intake

What are you grateful for today?

How do you feel today?

🙂 🙁 😫 😯 😭 😠

Why do you feel this way?

Rate your day!

TASK PLANNER

S M T W T F S
◯ ◯ ◯ ◯ ◯ ◯ ◯

DATE:

TASKS

- _____
- _____
- _____
- _____
- _____
- _____
- _____
- _____
- _____
- _____
- _____
- _____

PRIORITIES

NOTES

DAILY DIARY

DATE: _____

S M T W T F S
○ ○ ○ ○ ○ ○ ○

Today's Meals

- ....
- ....
- ....
- ....

What did you learn today?

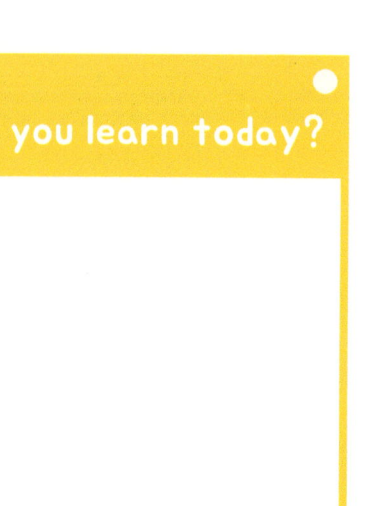

Water intake

What are you grateful for today?

How do you feel today?

😊 🙁 😫 😯 😭 😠

Why do you feel this way?

Rate your day!

☆ ☆ ☆ ☆ ☆

TASK PLANNER

S M T W T F S
○ ○ ○ ○ ○ ○ ○

DATE:

TASKS

- _____
- _____
- _____
- _____
- _____
- _____
- _____
- _____
- _____
- _____
- _____
- _____

PRIORITIES

NOTES

DAILY DIARY

DATE: _____

S M T W T F S
○ ○ ○ ○ ○ ○ ○

Today's Meals

○----------------○
○----------------○
○----------------○
○----------------○

What did you learn today?

Water intake

What are you grateful for today?

How do you feel today?

Why do you feel this way?

Rate your day!

TASK PLANNER

S M T W T F S
○ ○ ○ ○ ○ ○ ○

DATE:

TASKS

- _____
- _____
- _____
- _____
- _____
- _____
- _____
- _____
- _____
- _____

PRIORITIES

NOTES

DAILY DIARY

DATE:

S M T W T F S
○ ○ ○ ○ ○ ○ ○

Today's Meals

What did you learn today?

Water intake

What are you grateful for today?

How do you feel today?

Why do you feel this way?

Rate your day!

MONTHLY PLANNER

MONTH _____ **YEAR** _____

SUN	MON	TUE	WED	THU	FRI	SAT

TO-DO LIST

MONTHLY GOALS

WEEKLY PLANNER

WEEK _____   **MONTH** _____

SUNDAY	
MONDAY	
TUESDAY	
WEDNESDAY	
THURSDAY	
FRIDAY	
SATURDAY	

TO DO LIST
-
-
-
-
-
-
-
-
-

TASK PLANNER

S M T W T F S
○ ○ ○ ○ ○ ○ ○

DATE :

TASKS

- _____
- _____
- _____
- _____
- _____
- _____
- _____
- _____
- _____
- _____

PRIORITIES

NOTES

DAILY DIARY

DATE: _____

S M T W T F S
○ ○ ○ ○ ○ ○ ○

Today's Meals

What did you learn today?

Water intake

What are you grateful for today?

How do you feel today?

Why do you feel this way?

Rate your day!

TASK PLANNER

S M T W T F S
○ ○ ○ ○ ○ ○ ○

DATE :

TASKS

- ----------------------
- ----------------------
- ----------------------
- ----------------------
- ----------------------
- ----------------------
- ----------------------
- ----------------------
- ----------------------
- ----------------------
- ----------------------
- ----------------------

PRIORITIES

NOTES

DAILY DIARY

DATE: _____

S M T W T F S
○ ○ ○ ○ ○ ○ ○

What did you learn today?

Today's Meals

- - - - - - - - - - - - - - - - - - - -
- - - - - - - - - - - - - - - - - - - -
- - - - - - - - - - - - - - - - - - - -
- - - - - - - - - - - - - - - - - - - -

Water intake

What are you grateful for today?

How do you feel today?

🙂 🙁 😫 😯 😭 😠

Why do you feel this way?

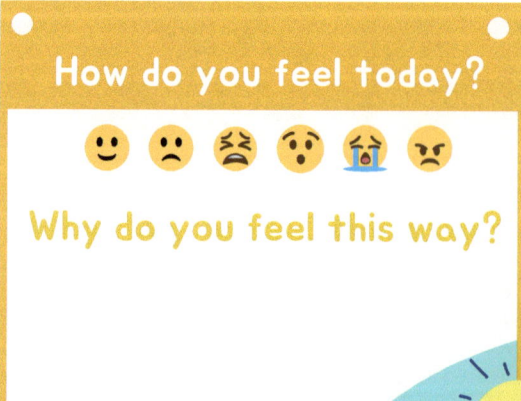

Rate your day!

TASK PLANNER

S M T W T F S
○ ○ ○ ○ ○ ○ ○

DATE :

TASKS

- _____
- _____
- _____
- _____
- _____
- _____
- _____
- _____
- _____
- _____
- _____

PRIORITIES

NOTES

DAILY DIARY

DATE: _____

S M T W T F S
○ ○ ○ ○ ○ ○ ○

Today's Meals

- ----------
- ----------
- ----------
- ----------

What did you learn today?

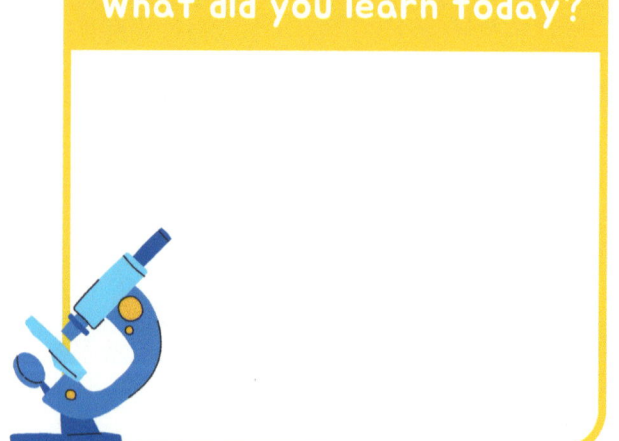

Water intake

What are you grateful for today?

How do you feel today?

🙂 🙁 😖 😯 😭 😠

Why do you feel this way?

Rate your day!

☆ ☆ ☆ ☆ ☆

TASK PLANNER

S M T W T F S
○ ○ ○ ○ ○ ○ ○

DATE:

TASKS

- _____
- _____
- _____
- _____
- _____
- _____
- _____
- _____
- _____
- _____
- _____
- _____

PRIORITIES

NOTES

DAILY DIARY

DATE :

S M T W T F S
○ ○ ○ ○ ○ ○ ○

Today's Meals

What did you learn today?

Water intake

What are you grateful for today?

How do you feel today?

Why do you feel this way?

Rate your day!

TASK PLANNER

S M T W T F S
○ ○ ○ ○ ○ ○ ○

DATE:

TASKS

- _____
- _____
- _____
- _____
- _____
- _____
- _____
- _____
- _____
- _____
- _____
- _____

PRIORITIES

NOTES

DAILY DIARY

DATE:

S M T W T F S
○ ○ ○ ○ ○ ○ ○

Today's Meals

What did you learn today?

Water intake

What are you grateful for today?

How do you feel today?

Why do you feel this way?

Rate your day!

TASK PLANNER

S M T W T F S
○ ○ ○ ○ ○ ○ ○

DATE:

TASKS

- _____
- _____
- _____
- _____
- _____
- _____
- _____
- _____
- _____
- _____
- _____

PRIORITIES

NOTES

DAILY DIARY

DATE: _____

S M T W T F S
○ ○ ○ ○ ○ ○ ○

Today's Meals

- - - - - - - - - - - - - - - -
- - - - - - - - - - - - - - - -
- - - - - - - - - - - - - - - -
- - - - - - - - - - - - - - - -

What did you learn today?

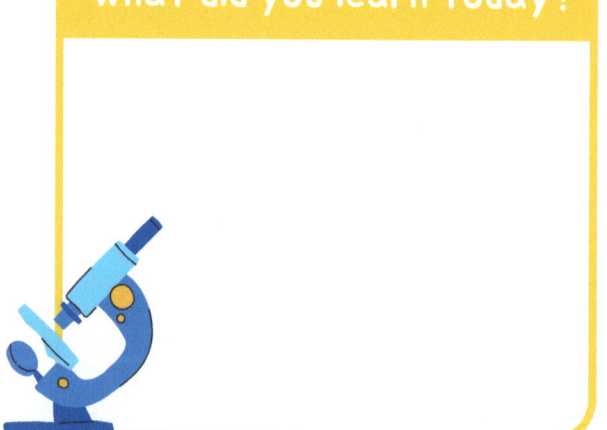

Water intake

What are you grateful for today?

How do you feel today?

🙂 🙁 😫 😯 😭 😠

Why do you feel this way?

Rate your day!

⭐ ⭐ ⭐ ⭐ ⭐

TASK PLANNER

S M T W T F S
○ ○ ○ ○ ○ ○ ○

DATE :

TASKS

- _____
- _____
- _____
- _____
- _____
- _____
- _____
- _____
- _____
- _____

PRIORITIES

NOTES

DAILY DIARY

DATE: _____

S M T W T F S
○ ○ ○ ○ ○ ○ ○

Today's Meals

What did you learn today?

Water intake

What are you grateful for today?

How do you feel today?
🙂 🙁 😣 😯 😭 😠

Why do you feel this way?

Rate your day!

ASSIGNMENT TRACKER

Subject	Task	Due Date	Status

New Year, New Goals!

Motivation Corner

(For when the going gets tough)

- Don't compare yourself and your achievements to others

- Focus on your own improvement and look back on how far you've come

- Reward yourself for finishing tasks

- Start with small tasks to feel a sense of accomplishment.

Motivation Corner

(For when the going gets tough)

- Face hard tasks head on

- Manage your expectations and avoid putting too much pressure on yourself

- Try to focus on the importance of education for your future

- Take a break when you feel overwhelmed

CAN YOU SPOT THE DIFFERENCES BETWEEN THE TW PHOTOS?

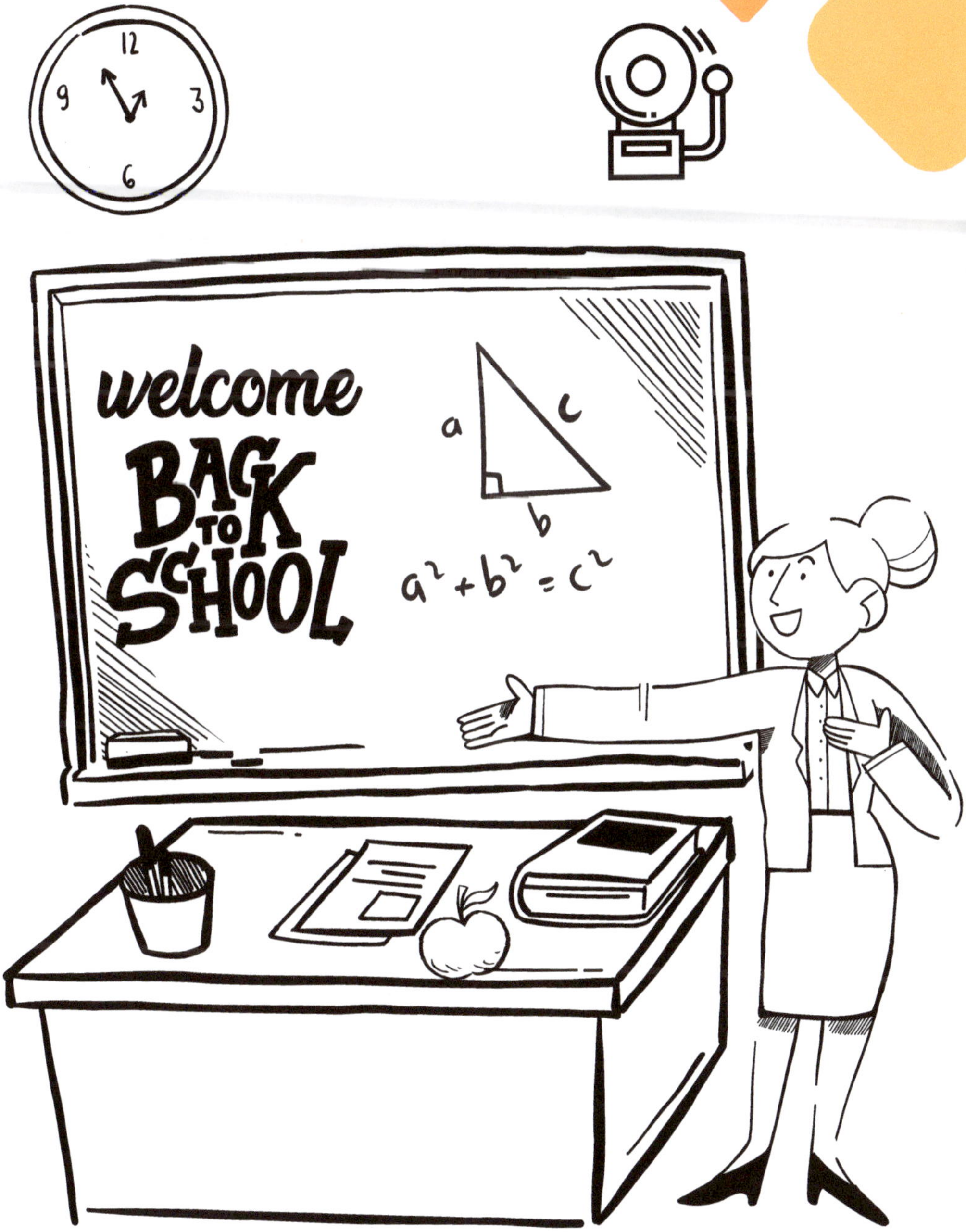

12
9
3
6
welcome
BACK TO SCHOOL
a
c
b
a² + b² = c²

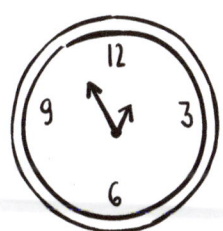

Copyright© 2022 by Bookfly Publishing

No part of this publication may be reproduced, stored in a retrieval system, or transmitted in any form or by any means, electronic, mechanical, photocopying, recording, or otherwise, without the written permission of the publisher. Limited Liability/Disclaimer of Warranty. The publisher and the author make no representation or warranties with the respect to the accuracy or completeness of the contents of this work and specifically disclaim all warranties including without limitation warranties for a particular purpose. No warranty may be created or extended by sales or promotional materials. The advice or strategies contained herein may not be suitable for every situation. This work is sold with the understanding that the publisher is not engaged in rendering medical, legal, or other professional advice or services. Neither the publisher nor the author or creator shall be liable for damages arising.

For general information on our other products and services please visit www.bookflypublishing.com or contact our Customer Care Department at info@bookflypublishing.com.
Bookfly Publishing publishes its books and materials in a variety of electronic and print formats. Some content that appears in print may not be available in electronic books and vice versa.

ISBN 978-1-7369393-5-2
All rights reserved. Published by Bookfly Publishing
Harvey, Louisiana
www.bookflypublishing.com

Printed in the USA

www.ingramcontent.com/pod-product-compliance
Lightning Source LLC
Chambersburg PA
CBHW040025130526
44590CB00037B/94